Featherstone

fantastic ideas for
creative role play

HAYLEY HUGHES

Featherstone
An imprint of Bloomsbury Publishing Plc

50 Bedford Square   1385 Broadway
London   New York
WC1B 3DP   NY 10018
UK   USA

www.bloomsbury.com

FEATHERSTONE and the Feather logo are trademarks of Bloomsbury Publishing Plc

First published in Great Britain 2017

Copyright © Hayley Hughes, 2017
Photos copyright © Hayley Hughes, 2017 / © Shutterstock 2017

Hayley Hughes has asserted her right under the Copyright, Designs and Patents Act, 1988,
to be identified as Author of this work.

Every reasonable effort has been made to trace copyright holders of material reproduced in this book, but if
any have been inadvertently overlooked the publishers would be glad to hear from them.

All rights reserved.
No part of this publication may be reproduced or transmitted in any form or by any means, electronic or
mechanical, including photocopying, recording, or any information storage or retrieval system, without prior
permission in writing from the publishers.

No responsibility for loss caused to any individual or organization acting on or refraining from action as a
result of the material in this publication can be accepted by Bloomsbury or the author.

A catalogue record for this book is available from the British Library.

ISBN
PB: 978-1-4729-4084-1
ePDF: 978-1-4729-4083-4

2 4 6 8 10 9 7 5 3 1

Printed and bound in India by Replika Press Pvt. Ltd.

This book is produced using paper that is made from wood grown in managed, sustainable forests. It is
natural, renewable and recyclable. The logging and manufacturing processes conform to the environmental
regulations of the country of origin.

To find out more about our authors and books visit www.bloomsbury.com. Here you will find extracts,
author interviews, details of forthcoming events and the option to sign up for our newsletters.

Acknowledgements

I wish to personally thank the headteachers Louise Moore and Tessa Smith and deputy headteacher Jane
Parker-Hack at Berwick Hills Primary School for enabling and inspiring me to develop my passion for play-
based learning. I would also like to thank all the children I have taught at Berwick Hills Primary School over
the years who have all been a delight to teach, and a special thanks to the parents too.

A special 'thank you' to Emma Pearson, Debbie Young, Tracy Watson, Karen Gale, Emma Duffy, Lyn
Cooper, Katrina Boyce, Joanne Munroe, Rachel Rees, Julie Shepherd, Hannah Johnson, Siama Ahmed,
Jessica Ditch, Lindsey Graham, Joseph Berry, Frankie Lee, Sue Sheperia, Zahra Shan, Liz Simpson and
Rebecca Cacioppo for their invaluable help supporting and creating the role play areas within this book. To
my closest friends Rebecca Cacioppo and Jo Vollands-Ross thank you for helping me to stay positive and
giving me amazing advice. And finally, to my husband, Simon, my parents and my two daughters Charlie
and Elise for having the patience with me for taking up a challenge, which took away some of the time I
could spend with them. Throughout the process of creating the role play areas, they have put up with my
endless crazy ideas and mess but never stopped encouraging and supporting me to achieve my dreams.

Contents

Introduction

I have been the Foundation Stage leader at Berwick Hills Primary School, Middlesborough for six years, working within Nursery and Reception classes. On arrival at the school I started to develop my passion for play-based learning, creating many different role play areas, which transformed the way the children interacted and learned. They were able to explore environments which developed their creative thinking skills through exploring and investigating. The infinite range of new and exciting things to discover and explore stimulated the children's curiosity and encouraged them to develop their learning further.

Throughout the past few years other teachers in my school, teaching assistants and myself have continued to experiment and to develop an outstanding early years environment to support the children in their learning.

This book will demonstrate how to create stimulating role play areas not just to inspire an exciting sense of awe and wonder, but also as a way of channeling the children's creativity and imagination through acting out different scenarios, to solve mysteries and problems. I hope this will help other practitioners to develop inspirational role play areas in their own settings.

The importance of the early years environment

In order to raise the status of play-based learning it is essential to create inspiring role play areas. Children develop their language skills directly through play. Play opportunities should be rich, inspiring and directly link to the children's interests in order for them to develop their imaginations.

Introducing a 'WOW' starting point means children can be introduced to an awe-inspiring scenario or problem that directly relies on their input and creative thinking. The practitioner can listen and respond to the children's ideas and opinions. Who knows where these scenarios could lead?

Creating a role play area

Every role play area has unlimited possibilities for children and adults to take on different roles, initiate ideas and directly respond to others' ideas. If you provide reading and writing materials within each area, children can also develop and practise key literacy skills. It is important for children to feel safe, happy and secure in any setting. Small, communication-friendly areas can help with this and can be easily set up by using small child-size gazebos, parasols and other play structures. Cover them in a range of materials using different colours and designs to suit your current topics.

Don't let the limitations and restrictions for developing role play outside put you off! You can provide themed boxes which can be used indoors or outdoors e.g. you could provide the children with a themed box to become a different person for the session. In the box there could be an outfit or costume, props that the person would use, writing resources, photographs, sound buttons, CD, books, labels and signs to create a quick and instant role play area.

The role of the practitioner

You should set up the role play scenario and then model and demonstrate the play, as this will initially support the children and encourage rich new language and key vocabulary. You then need to extend and challenge the children's creative thinking by using high quality focused open-ended questioning. You can also support children's play by creating and setting up different scenarios for children to take the lead and for them to decide what happens next e.g. helping a visitor or solving a problem.

Assessment, recording and reporting.

There are many references to role play in the early years curriculum and it's important therefore, that role play opportunities are available for every child and geared towards their interests: 'Children represent their own ideas, thoughts and feelings through design and technology, art, music, dance, role play and stories.' Children's play experiences should be recorded, monitored and next steps need to be planned so practitioners can help children move forward in their learning. After completing observations of the children using a role play area, you should adjust your plans accordingly

and if necessary carry out changes to enhance the children's learning. You should question whether it's necessary to add new resources, provide more modeling or introduce a different scenario.

The structure of the book

The pages are all organised in the same way. Before you start any activity, read through everything on the page so you are familiar with the whole activity and what you might need to plan in advance.

What you need lists the resources required for the activity. These are likely to be readily available in most settings or can be bought

What to do tells you step-by-step what you need to do to compete the activity.

Top tips give a brief suggestion or piece of advice to help in tackling the individual activity – these are things we wish we had known before we did them!

The **Health & Safety** tips are often obvious, but safety can't be overstressed. In many cases there are no specific hazards involved in completing the activity, and your usual health and safety measures should be enough. In others there are particular issues to be noted and addressed.

Taking it forward gives ideas for additional activities on the same theme, or for developing the activity further. These will be particularly useful for things that have gone especially well or where children show a real interest. In many cases they use the same resources, and in every case they have been designed to extend learning and broaden the children's experiences.

Finally, **What's in it for the children?** tells you (and others) briefly how the suggested activities contribute to learning.

Spring

What you need:

- Fairy lights
- Flowers, plants, tree stumps
- Easter role play area made from small gazebo covered and decorated

Role play items such as:

- Plastic eggs, different sizes and colours
- Easter baskets
- Masks, hats
- Spring toy animals eg. chicks, rabbits, lambs
- Clipboards and writing materials

Non-fiction/fiction books such as:

- *Where's the Easter Bunny?* by Louis Shea
- *Seasons: Spring* by Stephanie Turnbull

Taking it forward

To extend their play suggest some problem-solving scenarios to the children, such as the Easter bunny has left lots of eggs for the children to sort; the birds need help to start building their nests for spring; the baby lambs need feeding.

What's in it for the children?

Children will develop reading and language skills, learn about traditions and share stories. This is also an opportunity for them to learn about life cycles.

Questions you could ask

- Which way can we sort the eggs?
- What do we need to help the birds build their nests?
- How can we feed the lambs? What will you need?

Health & Safety

Ensure the children wash their hands after handling live animals.

What to do:

1. Introduce the theme of spring by surprising the children with an Easter egg hunt. Leave a note from the Easter bunny telling children he has left a very special egg which he has hidden. You could cut out bunny footprints for the children to follow around the setting to find the egg. Along the way, you could hide smaller eggs with hidden tasks such as 'complete ten bunny hops'!

2. Set up an investigation area called 'Easter Eggstravaganza' where the children can investigate lots of resources associated with spring. They could sort and match flowers and eggs of different sizes, colours and patterns. The children could take on the roles of different animals connected with spring such as lambs, rabbits and chicks.

Top tips

Send invitations home inviting the children to take part in an Easter bonnet competition. Take the children on an Easter bonnet parade around the setting and judge the best bonnet.

Arrange for real eggs to incubate in your setting and hatch out for the children to investigate.

50 fantastic ideas for creative role play

What you need:

- Autumn role play area made from small gazebo covered in paper and decorated
- Tree stumps
- Leaves
- Fairy lights
- Straw
- Cardboard boxes

Role play items such as:
- Soft toy woodland animals
- Pet carriers
- Feeding bottles and food bowls
- Pretend food
- Woodland animal masks
- Clipboards and writing materials

Non-fiction/fiction books such as:
- *Thinking about the Seasons: Autumn* by Clare Collinson
- *Autumn* by Ailie Busby

What to do:

1. Introduce the reading area by 'receiving' some toy hedgehogs in a pet carrier with care instructions. Tell the children that they need to feed the hedgehogs first, following the care instruction sheet. Then help the children to prepare a new home for the hedgehogs. They need to make the home by the end of October so the hedgehogs can hibernate over the winter. Encourage the children to read quietly in this area to avoid waking the hedgehogs.

2. Provide animal masks for the children to play with. They could act out stories based around animals that live in woodlands. The animals would need to find food and shelter as well as hide from predators.

3. Encourage the children to investigate the different woodland animals using non-fiction books.

Top tip ★

Organise clipboards and writing materials for the children to search for key words in the reading books and record what they find.

Taking it forward

To extend the children's play suggest some problem-solving scenarios such as a predator (badger) is following the squirrels; a badger's habitat has flooded; fox cubs have wandered away from their den and lost their mum.

What's in it for the children?

This is a great role play area for children to develop their reading and language development. They can handle books, share stories and interact with other children. They will also develop their understanding of woodland animals.

Questions you could ask

- How can we help keep the badger away from the squirrels?
- What could we do to help make a new habitat for the badger?
- Can you help the fox cubs? What can you do?

Winter

What you need:

- Winter role play area made from small gazebo covered in paper and decorated
- Tree stumps
- Pretend snow, snowflakes
- Shredded paper
- Painted pinecones
- Fairy lights

Role play items such as:

- Hats, gloves, scarves, wellies
- Fishing pool
- Fishing rods
- Torches
- Soft and plastic toy animals
- Animal masks
- Clipboards and writing materials
- Dressing-up costumes such as the White Witch and Jack Frost

Non-fiction/fiction books such as:

- *Popcorn: Seasons: Winter* by Kay Barnham
- *Is that you, Winter?* by Stephen Gammell

What to do:

1. Introduce the winter topic with Sidney the Snowman. Explain to the children that you have found him outside with a frozen rabbit called Reg. Show the children a soft toy animal that has been left in the freezer overnight. Ask the children what has happened to him and what they could do to help him. The children could then design and make a home for him.

2. Provide a range of winter clothing for the children to explore. They can get dressed ready for the cold weather.

3. A fishing pool can also be added for the children to explore and make direct links to number by 'catching' a number of fish.

4. The role of the White Witch could also be introduced. The Witch could take control of the land and keep everything frozen. The children could come up with ideas to save the wonderland from the evil Witch.

Taking it forward

The children could be presented with different scenarios to help solve, such as the pool has frozen and the penguins can't get any fish to eat; someone has stolen all the hats, gloves and scarves; the White Witch is turning everyone into stone.

What's in it for the children?

The winter role play areas are fantastic for the children to develop their knowledge and understanding of the world, and problem solving skills. They can find out new facts about the winter.

Questions you could ask

- How can we help the penguins find some fish?
- What shall we do without the hats, scarves and gloves?
- What should we do to stop the White Witch?

✚ Health & Safety

Ensure the children move safely when outside during cold conditions.

Top tips ⭐

Paint the tree stumps and pinecones with white paint to look like snow.

Farm

What you need:

- Barn role play area made from wooden play structure, covered with straw and brick material
- Cow print material
- Tuff tray with straw
- Cow made from cardboard boxes and paper
- Tractor made from cardboard boxes and decorated

Role play items such as:

- Role play costumes such as vets, farmers, animals
- Clipboards and writing materials
- Wellies
- Straw bales, fencing
- Seeds
- Farm toy animals
- Animal food
- Spades, rakes, watering cans
- Plants

Non-fiction/fiction books such as:

- *Animals on the Farm* by Lark Books

What's in it for the children?

The children will develop their communication and language skills by suggesting ways to solve problems, initiating ideas and then responding to what others are saying. The children will develop their understanding of the natural world and discuss the things they find out about the animals on the farm.

Questions you could ask

- How can we help the animals find their way home?
- How can we fix the tractor?
- Who can help the pig?

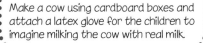

Top tip ⭐

Make a cow using cardboard boxes and attach a latex glove for the children to imagine milking the cow with real milk.

What to do:

1. Introduce the farm topic by organising the arrival of some eggs to hatch, or visit a real farm.

2. Provide the children with a special pet carrier complete with instructions for how to look after a baby lamb. Explain that the baby lamb needs help to become stronger before it can be returned to the farm. The children will need to feed it with a bottle and keep it warm.

3. Using the farm role play area, the children can take on the role of a farmer. They could feed the animals, plant seeds, round up the animals, look after the crops, milk the cows and ride the tractor. They could also take on the role of the farm animals. The animals could even become sick and then a vet would be needed to help.

Taking it forward

To extend the children's play, they could be given problem-solving scenarios such as the animals have escaped from the field; the tractor has stopped working and it's stuck in a field; a pig is poorly.

Farm shop

What you need:

- Farm shop role play areas made from den structure and small gazebo
- Cardboard
- Straw
- Stencil cut-outs of different animal footprints

Role play items such as:

- Weighing scales
- A toy till and money
- Telephone
- Shopping and presentation baskets
- Egg boxes, milk cartons
- Pretend food such a meat, fruit and vegetables, eggs
- Dressing-up costumes such as farmer, shopkeeper
- Clipboards and writing materials

Non-fiction/fiction books such as:

- *Food From Farms (World of Farming)* by Nancy Dickmann
- *Where Does the Food We Eat Come From?* by Rami Erez

What to do:

1. Prepare the farm shop by leaving a trail of muddy animal foot prints. When the children arrive, surprise them by taking a pretend phone call to inform them that some local farm animals have stolen all the food. Let the children see the trail of footprints and ask them to identify which footprint belongs to which animal such as pig, chicken or sheep dog. Let the children investigate and suggest ways to solve this mystery. They could follow a trail that leads to the stolen food or the animals.

2. Invite the children to become the shopkeeper and pretend to order, weigh and sell the food. They could also take on the role of the customers and request and pay for different items, asking for the prices.

Taking it forward

To extend their play suggest some problem-solving scenarios to the children such as eggs have been delivered and all of them are cracked; the farmer is late with his delivery to the shop; the weighing scales are broken.

Top tip ⭐

Use brown clay to create animal footprints to make it look like they have just walked off the farm.

What's in it for the children?

The farm shop role play area can be used to develop the children's everyday language relating to counting and money. They could be encouraged to buy and sell a range of items, add up prices and give the correct change.

Questions you could ask

- What should we do with all the eggs?
- How can we contact the farmer?
- What will we do without the weighing scales?

✚ Health & Safety

If you choose to use real fruit and vegetables check the children have no allergies.

Dragons

What you need:

- Castle role play area made from cardboard sheet and painted
- Handwritten letter from Dorothy the Dragon explaining her dilemma

Role play items such as:

- Soft toy dragons
- Cardboard box cage
- Fake medicine bottles
- Swords
- Treasure
- Dragon eggs
- Dressing-up costumes such as knights, princes and princesses, king and queens - and dragons!
- Clipboards and writing materials

Non-fiction/fiction books such as:

- *There's No Such Thing as a Dragon* by Jack Kent
- *The Dragon with a Big Nose* by Kathy Henderson

What to do:

1. Introduce the topic of dragons by telling the children you found a cage with a special visitor inside – ask them if they would like to see her? Reveal the cage and read the letter written by Dorothy the Dragon explaining that her throat is sore because she keeps breathing too much fire and burning all the houses around her. Tell the children she is a friendly dragon and only wants to make friends with the people where she lives but they are all frightened of her. Explain the Great Master Dragon has given her some magic medicine to heal her throat but she's not very good at measuring it out. Can the children help her find out how much the medicine bottles hold?

2. Encourage the children to act out scenarios where they are a king, queen, prince, princess, knight or a dragon. They could experience protecting the prince or princess in the tower, guarding the treasure or becoming a knight and having a pretend sword fight with a dragon to determine the winner.

> **Top tip** ⭐
>
> Invite parents into the setting to help celebrate the topic of dragons. They could support the children by taking part in dragon-themed activities.

Taking it forward

My name is Dorothy.

To extend their play suggest some problem-solving scenarios to the children such as: crossing a moat without the dragon hearing them; the dragon has laid eggs overnight; the prince/princess is trapped with no food.

What's in it for the children?

The children will develop their understanding of life in the past and can discuss the things they learned about castles.

Questions you could ask

- How can we move over the bridge quietly?
- What should we do with the eggs?
- How can we help the prince/princess?

Dinosaur

What you need:

- Dinosaur-land made from a small gazebo
- Cut out leaves and crêpe paper vines, dinosaur silhouettes
- Large tray and stand with shredded paper
- Tree stumps, sand, sticks and logs
- Dinosaur themed decorations and materials

Role play items such as:

- An assortment of toy dinosaurs
- Dressing-up clothes such as dinosaur, archaeologist, caveman
- Paper mâché dinosaur eggs
- Fossils made from clay imprints
- Brushes, spades, sieves
- Magnifying glasses
- Torches
- Clipboards and writing materials

Non-fiction/fiction books such as:

- National Geographic Little Kids: *First Big Book of Dinosaurs*
- *Ten Little Dinosaurs* by Mike Brownlow and Simon Rickerty

What to do:

1. Have 'dinosaur eggs' delivered 'from the museum' for the children to explore and look after. The eggs could arrive with a special letter with instructions for the children explaining how to look after them. Let the children decide how to care for them. Provide magnifying glasses to observe them hatching over time. They could crack open a little every day to create excitement. Help the children to make a nest for the eggs to hatch in.

2. Have a dinosaur day. Start the day by taking the children taking part in a 'Dinormous' treasure hunt around the whole setting following footprints … you could even dress up as an enormous dinosaur as their leader!

3. Play 'dinosaur pass the parcel', 'pin the tail on the stegosaurus', 'pass the hot fossil', 'steal the egg from the sleeping dinosaur', 'throw the dinosaur bone into the bin', 'dinosaur musical bumps', 'dinosaur egg and spoon race' and not forgetting 'dancing like your favourite dinosaur'!

4. Prepare 'Dinormous' party food in a themed 'Dinosaur land' room. Ask the children to help make party decorations: printed tablecloths, place mats and hats. Add shredded paper and toy dinosaurs as centre pieces to complete an ideal party room. Let the children help you to make dinosaur jelly, sandwiches, cakes and biscuits. Make your party fit for any dinosaur or caveman to enjoy.

Top tips ⭐

Create homemade fossils and dinosaur bones using salt dough and clay.

To make the dinosaur eggs, hide toys inside balloons, blow them up and then cover with papier mache ready to hatch out.

5. For party costumes, make simple dinosaur hats with the children. The practitioners can dress up too. You can make dinosaur and caveman costumes out of old clothes, paper and cardboard.

6. After the party, present the children with a thank you card for taking part in the best 'Dinormous' party ever!

7. Send questionnaires home to find out if your party has been a 'roaring' success.

8. Encourage the children to name, describe and act out scenarios with the different dinosaurs. They could pretend to be a caveman or a dinosaur moving quickly or slowly around the area depending on the species.

9. Develop a 'dinosaur dig' area where the children could take on the role of an archaeologist and hunt for dinosaur fossils and bones. Encourage the children to discuss, describe and record their findings.

10. Set up a small world play area with plastic dinosaurs hidden in coloured water with twigs, straw and bark to look like a dinosaur swamp.

Taking it forward

To extend their play, suggest some problem-solving scenarios to the children such as one of the dinosaur eggs hasn't cracked open; the caveman can't find anything to eat; a dinosaur is poorly.

What's in it for the children?

These are great role play areas for children to develop their language skills. They will interact with other children, initiate ideas and explore making up stories.

Questions you could ask

- Why do you think the egg hasn't cracked open?
- How can we help the caveman find something to eat?
- What can we do to make the dinosaur feel better?

✚ Health & Safety

Ensure the sand is changed regularly and children wash their hands after use.

Fairies

What you need:

- A handwritten letter from a fairy explaining she has a broken wing and needs the children's help
- Small world fairy area made using a decorated parasol
- An assortment of woodland decorations such as bark, pine cones, flower petals, toy toadstools etc.
- Glitter
- Fishing nets
- Small toy fairies
- Clipboards and writing materials
- Dressing-up costumes for fairies, elves

Non-fiction/fiction books such as:

- *The Real Fairy Storybook* by Emma Chambers
- *That's Not My Fairy* by Fiona Watt

What to do:

1. Whilst using the outside area the children could find a tiny letter and a fairy with a broken wing. The letter tells the children that the fairy broke her wing on the branch of a tree. Can the children help the fairy make a new fairyland for her to recover in? First they need to catch as much fairy dust as possible to include in their fairyland. Show the children the fishing nets and throw glitter in the air for the children to catch in their nets.

2. Help the children to make a small world fairyland using woodland materials and don't forget to include the magic pot of fairy dust to help the fairy get better.

3. Let the children take on the roles of giant fairies, or elves. They could go on adventures, have magical powers and help solve different mysteries.

Top tip ★

Place a trail of glitter leading up to and around the fairy's letter to create more excitement.

Taking it forward

To extend their play suggest some problem-solving scenarios to the children, such as the fairies have lost their magical powers; one of the fairy's wands is missing; the fairies can't fly.

What's in it for the children?

The children will develop their communication and language skills by suggesting ways to solve problems, initiating ideas and then responding to what others are saying.

Questions you could ask

- How can you help the fairies get back their magical powers?
- Who do you think has stolen the wand?
- What can we do to help the fairies?

✚ Health & Safety

Make sure the children are carefully supervised when using small objects which could present a choking hazard.

Jungle

What you need:

- Jungle role play area made from small gazebo covered in paper and decorated
- Paper leaves and vines
- Tuff tray

Role play items such as:

- An assortment of toy jungle animals
- Dressing-up costumes for explorers, jungle animals
- Backpack explore kits with:
  - Magnifying glasses
  - Jungle passports
  - Compasses
  - Binoculars
  - Maps
- Clipboards and writing materials

Non-fiction/fiction books such as:

- *Jungle books for Kids: Scary Animals of the Jungle* by Baby Professor
- *Down in the Jungle* by Elisa Squillace

What to do:

1. Introduce the jungle topic by organising an explorer's backpack. Let the children open the backpack and discover an explorer's kit and instructions for a jungle exhibition. Guide them as they follow the clues and banana skin trail (set up earlier) to find a greedy gorilla called Graham.

2. The children could pass through different animal areas around the setting such as 'monkey mayhem', the snake swamp, crocodile creek and the lion's lair. The children could even experience passing a talking parrot who gives them a clue about where Graham is hiding.

3. Model and demonstrate a range of jungle scenarios. The children could pretend they are the animals found in the jungle, hunt for food and make shelters. Alternatively, they might become explorers.

4. Set up a small world play jungle land with plastic jungle animals and fencing for the children to discover.

Taking it forward

To extend their play suggest some problem-solving scenarios such as the children have been given an opportunity to adopt a monkey; the explorer has lost his jungle map and needs help finding her/his way out; the explorer has found an enormous bone.

Top tip ★

Make pretend tiki torches using bamboo canes, cardboard and tissue paper.

What's in it for the children?

The children will develop their understanding of the natural world and will develop their ability to talk about the things they learn about the animals that live in the jungle.

Questions you could ask

- How can we find out what the monkey needs?
- What should the explorer do with the bone? Who does it belong to?

Garden

What you need:

- Garden centre role play area made from wooden play structure
- Netting
- Flowers
- Reading garden made from small gazebo

Role play items such as:

- Plants, flowers, herbs
- Dressing-up costumes for shopkeepers, customers
- A toy till and money
- Price lists, catalogues, an order book
- Telephone
- Seed packets, bulbs
- Gardening tools such as watering cans, buckets, seed trays, flower pots and a wheelbarrow
- Clipboards and writing materials

Non-fiction/fiction books such as:

- *Peep Inside the Garden* by Anna Milbourne
- *My First Book of Garden Bugs* by Mike Unwin

Taking it forward

To extend their play suggest some problem-solving scenarios to the children such as a customer has stolen some flowers; a customer has lost their purse and doesn't know how to pay; the rabbits have dug up the plants.

What's in it for the children?

The garden centre role play area develops the children's everyday language relating to money and numbers. They will be encouraged to buy and sell a range of items, add up prices and give the correct change.

Questions you could ask

- What are you going to say to the lady who stole the flowers?
- How can you help the lady who has lost her purse?

What to do:

1. Set the scene: a mysterious large box has arrived. Inside the box a kind person has donated some resources for them to set up their own role play area. At the bottom of the box the children discover there is a big hole. All of the donations must have fallen out as it was delivered! The children must find different objects around the outside or inside the setting that have fallen out of the box.

2. In the garden centre the children could take on the role of a shopkeeper or customer. They can buy and sell a range of items. The shopkeeper can give customers advice about what to grow and how to grow it. They might take orders, telephone calls and make deliveries. The customer can ask questions about the different products and purchase items.

3. For the reading part of the garden provide animal masks for the children to explore. They could act out stories based around animals that live in the garden. Encourage the children to investigate the different animals using the non-fiction books.

Top tip ⭐

Let the children make flowers to decorate and use in the garden centre.

➕ **Health & Safety**

If children are touching soil ensure they wear protective gloves.

Flower shop

What you need:

- Flower shop role play area made from plastic greenhouse
- Trellis (optional) and flowers
- A teddy bear

Role play items such as:

- Shopping baskets
- A toy till and money
- Price lists, catalogues, an order book
- Telephone
- Message cards
- Wrapping paper
- Flowerpots
- Clipboards and writing materials

Non-fiction/fiction books such as:

- *First Book of Flowers* by Anita Ganeri
- *A Seed in Need: A First Look at the Plant Cycle* by Sam Godwin

What to do:

1. Show the children Tina the Teddy who is very sad. Explain to the children that she was all ready for her wedding day on Saturday and everything was fine until she had her flowers delivered. Show the children her snapped flowers (already prepared). As you have the flower shop in the setting help the children to think of ways in which they can help Tina so that she can still have her special day.

2. In the flower shop the children could take on the role of the shopkeeper or the customer. They can buy and sell a range of items. The shopkeeper can give the customers advice about what flowers they would like. They might create bouquets for birthdays, weddings or even Valentine's day. They could take orders, telephone calls and make deliveries.

Taking it forward

To extend their play suggest some problem-solving scenarios to the children such as: the flowers have been left with no water; the delivery van has forgotten the red flowers; a lady doesn't like her bouquet.

What's in it for the children?

The flower shop role play area develops the children's mathematical language. They will be encouraged to 'buy and sell' a range of items, add up prices and give the correct change.

Questions you could ask

- What can we do to help the flowers that have been left without water?
- How can we contact the delivery man?
- What should we say to the lady about her bouquet?

Top tip ⭐

Let the children make their own flowers to use in this area.

Minibeasts

What you need:

- Minibeast role play area made from small gazebo covered in paper and decorated
- Minibeast den made from pop up tent
- Tree stumps
- Artificial grass mat material
- Tuff tray
- Bark, stones
- A worm farm

Role play items such as:

- Dressing-up costumes for scientists, minibeasts
- Safety goggles
- Magnifying glasses
- Clipboards and writing materials

Non-fiction/fiction books such as:

- *Mad About Minibeasts!* by Giles Andreae
- *Nick Baker's Bug Book: Discover the World of the Mini-beast!* by Nick Baker

What to do:

1. For that extra 'wow' factor, introduce the topic by arranging a specialist company to bring in a selection of exotic minibeasts for the children to investigate. Follow this visit up with the children receiving a certificate from the company to say they think the children are the best experts they have ever seen. As the children are amazing, they need to set up the nation's first ever all-insect museum.

2. Help the children set up an investigation lab and a museum. The children could take on the role of an entomologist. They must work out how to describe and share their knowledge with visitors.

3. Set up woodland or garden dens to allow the children to take on the role of an explorer. The children could search for the minibeasts and describe and compare their similarities and differences.

4. Create a 'wormery' with the children and observe the changes that occur over time.

Top tip ⭐

Present the children with special white science lab coats and safety glasses to wear whilst playing in the lab and museum. This will create instant interest and excitement.

✚ Health & Safety

Ensure that the soil is not contaminated with any nasties and that the children wash their hands throroughly after exploring.

Taking it forward

To extend the play, suggest some problem-solving scenarios to the children, such as: someone has left the tops off the tanks and the minibeasts have escaped; the explorer is lost in the woodland without a torch; a giant butterfly has caught its wing on a branch of a tree.

What's in it for the children?

The children will develop their communication and language skills by suggesting ways to solve problems, initiating ideas and then responding to what others are saying.

Questions you could ask

- How can we find and catch all the missing minibeasts?
- What can we do to help the explorer?
- Is there any way we can help the butterfly?

Pets

What you need:

- Pet shop role play area made from play tent structure covered in paper and cardboard

Role play items such as:

- Dressing-up costumers such as vets, shopkeepers, customers
- Soft toy animals
- Pet food and bowls
- Pet carriers and cages
- Straw, hay
- Pet collars, leads and toys
- Shopping baskets
- Weighing scales
- A toy till and money
- Telephone
- Information leaflets
- Clipboards and writing materials

Non-fiction/fiction books such as:

- *Animals at the Pet Shop (Animals I Can See)* by Sian Smith
- *I Want A Pet* by Lauren Child

What to do:

1. Paint a sore wound on a soft toy animal found in the pet shop such as a guinea pig and the introduce the pets theme by saying you have a sick pet. Explain to the children that a guinea pig has become poorly and ask the children to suggest ways they could help make it better.

2. The children could take on the roles of the shopkeeper or customer. They could pretend to buy and sell the different animals and equipment. They will need to care for the animals in the pet shop, weigh out food, order more stock and write out bills and receipts. The children could also take on the role of a vet giving the animals routine injections, check-ups and treating any illnesses.

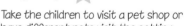

Top tip ★

Take the children to visit a pet shop or have different pets visit the setting.

Taking it forward

To extend their play, suggest some problem-solving scenarios to the children such as: the pet shop has had a phone call from a customer; a pet hamster is poorly; there is no more hay left in stock; a customer wants to buy a rabbit.

What's in it for the children?

The pet shop role play area develops the children's everyday language relating to money and numbers. They will be encouraged to buy and sell a range of items, add up prices and give the correct change.

Questions you could ask

- How can you help the poorly hamster?
- What should we do to get more hay?
- Can you tell the customer what they need to look after a rabbit?

✚ Health & Safety

Ensure children have no allergies to small animals before arranging a visit to a pet shop or zoo.

Rainforest

What you need:

- Rainforest café role play area made from small gazebo covered in paper and decorated
- Paper leaves and vines
- Children's small picnic table and chairs
- Rainforest foods for tasting eg. chocolate, avocados, pineapple

Role play items such as:

- Dressing-up costumes for chef, waiter/waitress, customers
- Plastic tea set
- Menu
- Play food
- Telephone
- Cooking pans
- Order forms
- Clipboards and writing materials

Non-fiction/fiction books such as:

- *Secrets in the Rainforest* by Carron Brown
- *A Walk in the Rainforest* by Kristin Joy Pratt-Serafini

What to do:

1. Introduce the area by showing the children a picture of the endangered rainforest. Explain to the children that we need to help save the animals and look after them here in our rainforest until it is safe for them to return. Tell the children there is no time to 'monkey around' they need to plan a meal for the animals that are coming to their rainforest. Encourage the children to think about what the animals eat and and prepare for their visit.

2. The children will need to discuss what role they need to take on while using the café. They could take orders, cook, and then serve the meals.

3. The children can explore the different foods that are associated with the rainforest. Organise different fruits for the children to taste that are associated with the rainforest such as coconuts, avocados and pineapples.

Top tip

Use animal print paper to cover the tables. Organise rainforest sound effects to play in the café.

Taking it forward

To extend their play suggest some problem-solving scenarios to the children such as: the food delivery hasn't turned up; the dishwasher has broken.

What's in it for the children?

This area will also provide opportunities for the children to learn new vocabulary and extend their language skills. They will develop everyday language relating to money and numbers.

Questions you could ask

- What should we do about the delivery not turning up?
- How can we fix the dishwasher?

Health & Safety

Ensure children have no allergies to different foods.

Polar regions

What you need:

- Polar Regions role play area made from small gazebo covered in paper and decorated
- Tuff tray
- Pretend snow and snowflakes

Role play items such as:

- Dressing-up costumes for explorers, polar animals
- Soft and plastic toy animals
- Clipboards and writing materials

Non-fiction/fiction books such as:

- *One Day on Our Blue Planet in the Antartic* by Ella Bailey
- *When the Sun Shines on Antarctica: And Other Poems about the Frozen Continent* by Irene Latham

Top tip

Put the animals in a clear container of water with cotton wool, sequins and glitter then freeze overnight.

Taking it forward

To extend their play suggest some problem-solving scenarios to the children such as: the room is too hot and the ice is melting; a baby penguin has lost her mother; there is no fish for the polar bears to eat.

What's in it for the children?

The children will develop their communication and language skills by suggesting ways to solve problems, initiating ideas and then responding to what others are saying. The children will develop their understanding of the natural world and will develop their ability to talk about the creatures that live in the polar regions.

Questions you could ask

- How can we stop the ice melting?
- Can you find the penguin's mother?
- Where can we get more fish?

What to do:

1. When introducing the theme of polar regions create awe and wonder: Santa's reindeer are visiting, and they've brought a sleigh full of penguins from Antarctica! Show the children a letter from Santa explaining to the children that they need to look after the animals, and encourage them to think of ways to keep them cold.

2. Invite the children to explore the polar areas. They could pretend to be the different animals living there. The children could also make an igloo for an arctic explorer to shelter in.

3. Organise a small world area with animals, ice and snow so children can explore the texture and use the animals to act out stories.

Santa's workshop

What you need:

- Santa's workshop role play area made from play tent structure covered in cardboard and painted
- Santa's sleigh made from a painted cardboard box

Role play items such as:

- Dressing-up costumes for Santa, elves
- Sacks
- Wrapping paper
- Broken toys to fix
- Pretend tools
- Clipboards and writing materials

Non-fiction/fiction books such as:

- *What Does Santa do on Boxing Day?* by Becky Plenderleith
- *That's Good! That's Bad! On Santa's Journey* by Margery Cuyler

Taking it forward

To extend their play suggest some problem-solving scenarios to the children such: as Santa leaves a sack full of objects to sort; the elves need help sorting the heavy and light presents to load on the sleigh; the presents have got muddled up and they have the wrong names on.

What's in it for the children?

The children will develop their communication and language skills by suggesting ways to solve problems, initiating ideas and then responding to what others are saying. They will also develop their physical skills by using the tools and equipment effectively.

Questions you could ask

- How do you know all those presents are the heavy ones?
- How shall we sort the presents?
- Is there anything we can do to fix the sleigh?

What to do:

1. Introduce the Christmas theme by unveiling Santa's footprints. The children follow them to find a big sack, a letter from Santa saying that the elves are really busy. In fact, they're *too* busy and need their help. Santa has left a few toys for them to fix. Show the children a few toys that have been broken that they could pretend to fix.

2. The children can take on the role of an elf or Santa. They can pretend to make toys using pretend tools. After making the toys they need wrapping, sorting and checking. The children will love to drive the sleigh and deliver all the presents.

Top tip

Make Santa snow footprints using a stencil and talc. Supply the children with Christmas photo booth props and let them pretend to be different people and have fun.

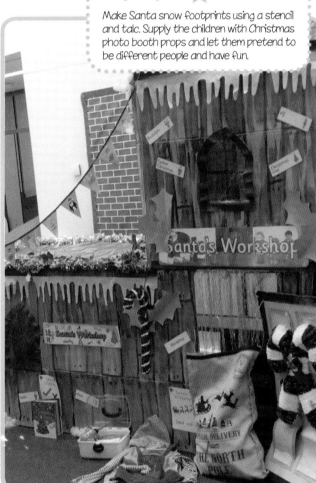

Bakery

What you need:

- Bakery role play area made from wooden play structure covered in paper and decorated

Role play items such as:

- Cake stands
- Cake cases
- Mixing bowls
- Whisks, mixing spoons
- Cooker
- Weighing scales
- Shopping baskets
- Pretend cakes, and ingredients
- A toy till and money
- Receipts, order forms
- Clipboards and writing materials
- Dressing-up costumes for bakers, customers

Non-fiction/fiction books such as:

- *Baker Cat* by Posy Simmonds
- *Happy Street: Bakery* by Simon Abbott

What to do:

1. The children receive a newspaper article advertising a 'Bake off'. The article states that a group of children is needed to bake cakes to raise money for their local park. The article informs them how to make the 'best' cakes by following the instructions to the letter. They must pretend to make as many cakes as possible. Tell the children that the mayor has sent Bruce the Baker as a judge and will decide which group is the winner. The winners will visit the local mayor's office to receive a special award certificate.

2. The children could pretend to make different cakes following instructions. Customers could order cakes for special occasions. The children will gain experience of making, buying and selling cakes, filling out order forms and receipts.

Top tip ⭐

Use cheap party decorations such as bunting and streamers to decorate the bakery.

Taking it forward

To extend their play suggest some problem-solving scenarios to the children such as: the oven timer didn't go off and the cake is burnt; a customer has not collected her cake; the order for butter hasn't arrived.

What's in it for the children?

The bakery shop role play area develops the children's everyday language relating to money and numbers. They will be encouraged to buy and sell a range of items, add up prices and give the correct change.

Questions you could ask

- What should we do with the burnt cake? What will the customer say?
- How can we tell the customer to collect her cake?
- What should we do about the butter delivery not turning up?

Chinese restaurant

What you need:

- Chinese restaurant role play area made from wooden play structure covered in paper and decorated

Role play items such as:

- Chinese lanterns and decorations
- Pans, woks
- Cups, plates
- Chopsticks
- Menu
- A toy till and money
- Play food
- Telephone
- Dressing-up costumes for chef, waiter/waitress, customers
- Clipboards and writing materials

Non-fiction/fiction books such as:

- *Chinese New Year* by Grace Jones
- *Lanterns and Firecrackers: A Chinese New Year Story* by Jonny Zucker

What's in it for the children?

The children will be introduced to a different culture. They will learn about new traditions and different foods. They will acquire new vocabulary associated with food and traditions to support their play.

Questions you could ask

- What could we say to the customer who is rude?
- Where can the customer whose table has been taken, sit?
- How can we cook the food if the cooker is broken?

Top tip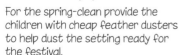

For the spring-clean provide the children with cheap feather dusters to help dust the setting ready for the festival.

What to do:

1. Why not create this area during the period of the Chinese New Year? It is a traditional holiday known as Spring Festival. To start the theme, ask the children to spring-clean the setting ready for the festival. Help the children decorate the area with red lanterns, lights and decorations. The children could then make dragon masks and take part in a dragon dance along to music. Red paper envelopes could be decorated with gold Chinese symbols and given out to the children. Arrange a special banquet for the children to experience Chinese food and traditions.

2. The children could take on the role of being the waiter or waitress, chef or customer in a Chinese restaurant. They might take phone calls to book tables, make orders, cook the food, serve or pretend to eat the food.

Taking it forward

To extend their play suggest some problem-solving scenarios to the children such as: a customer is rude to the waiter and spills her food on the floor; a customer has booked a table but it is already taken; the cooker has broken.

Indian restaurant

What you need:

- Indian restaurant role play area made from small gazebo covered in paper and decorated

Role play items such as:

- Ready-mixed paint
- Wooden logs
- Water balloons
- Play food
- Telephone
- Napkins, cutlery
- Pans, cups, plates
- Menu
- A toy till and money
- Dressing-up costumes for chef, waiter/waitress, customers
- Clipboards and writing materials

Non-fiction/fiction books such as:

- *Holi* by Lynn Peppas

Top tip ⭐

Ask the parents/carers to provide white coats or clothes they don't mind getting messy!

What's in it for the children?

The children will be introduced to a different culture. They will learn about new traditions and different foods. They will acquire new vocabulary associated with food and traditions to support their play.

Questions you could ask

- What should we do with the food that's too spicy?
- How can we put the fire out?
- How can we get more customers to visit?

➕ **Health & Safety**

Ensure children have no allergies to certain Indian foods or to the paint.

What to do:

1. To introduce this new role play area invite the children to celebrate the Holi festival. This takes place during spring and is the ancient Indian festival of colours. The children could start the celebration on the eve of Holi. They could make a pretend fire out of the logs and paper to get rid of any evil spirits. The children could wear white clothes, then as is traditional cover themselves in brightly coloured paint by throwing paint filled water balloons. Continue the festivities by presenting the children with a selection of Indian food to taste.

2. The children might take on the role of being the waiter or waitress, chef or customer in the Indian restaurant. They could take phone calls to book tables, make orders, cook the food, serve or pretend to eat the food.

Taking it forward

To extend their play suggest some problem-solving scenarios to the children such as: the chef has put too much spice in the food; the cooker has caught fire; there aren't enough customers coming to the restaurant.

Space

What you need:

- Spaceship structure made from large cardboard sheets covered in foil and decorated
- Tuff tray filled with gravel, shredded paper, stones, cotton wool and polystyrene pieces

Role play items such as:

- A teddy bear
- Suitcase/backpack filled with holiday gear eg. sunglasses, sun cream, swimsuit
- Cameras
- Aliens and space toys
- Space rocks
- Dressing-up costumes for astronauts, aliens
- Logbook
- Clipboards and writing materials

Non-fiction/fiction books such as:

- *What's Out There?* by Lynn Wilson
- *A Look at our Solar System* by D.L Madson

What to do:

1. Introduce the topic of space by meeting Super Sam the Ted. He has a problem; he wants to join his friend Steven on holiday but he's packed the wrong things. Show the children what Super Sam has packed in his suitcase: sun hat, sunglasses, swimsuit, sun cream. Sam thought he was going to sunny Spain! Oh no! He has got it all wrong! He is going to go somewhere even more special. He has been invited to go to the moon on a space rocket! Invite the children to help Super Sam the Ted become Super Sam the *Space* Ted and suggest what to wear to go to space (space suit, space helmet, space boots).

2. The children could take on the role of astronauts and aliens visiting friendly and hostile planets.

3. Small world space areas are ideal for children to experience space play using small astronaut and alien figures.

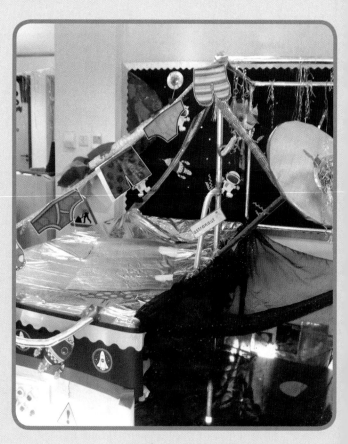

Top tip ⭐

The children could make space rocks out of clay using their fingers to create holes. A space land can then be created with sand, glitter and then rocks added for children to explore and sort according to their size and weight.

✚ Health & Safety

Ensure the children wash their hands after handling clay.

Taking it forward

To extend their play suggest some problem-solving scenarios to the children such as: a space ship has crash-landed onto the playground; an astronaut has a secret mission to find out about another planet; there is a dangerous alien on the loose in their setting.

What's in it for the children?

This is a great role play area for children to develop their language and communication skills. They will interact with other children, initiate ideas and explore making up stories and adding narrative into their play.

Questions you could ask

- What should we do about the space ship that has crash-landed in the playground?
- Why would you like to be the astronaut on a secret mission?
- Why do you think the alien has come to our school?

Supermarket

What you need:

- Supermarket role play area made from small gazebo covered in paper and decorated

Role play items such as:

- Shopping baskets/trolleys
- Toy till and money
- Phone
- Empty food boxes and containers
- Dressing-up costumes for shopkeepers, customers
- Clipboards and writing materials

Non-fiction/fiction books such as:

- *Supermarket (Busy Places)* by Carol Watson
- *Supermarket* by Kathleen Krull

What to do:

1. Create a grand supermarket opening by cutting a ribbon and inviting a special guest to open it. The visitor could bring a wrapped up present such as a small shopping trolley for the children, to help make their supermarket even more special.

2. The children can take on the role of a shopkeeper or customer. The shopkeeper would need to set up items to sell and write bills, orders and receipts. As a customer they could choose the food they would like to buy, calculate how much it costs, and pay.

Taking it forward

To extend their play suggest some problem-solving scenarios such as: the supermarket lights go off; a customer forgets to pay for their shopping; the till is stuck can't be opened.

What's in it for the children?

The supermarket role play areas will develop the children's everyday language relating to money and number. They can be encouraged to buy and sell a range of items, add up prices and give the correct change.

Questions you could ask

- How can we fix the lights?
- What should we do about the customer not paying?
- How can we help the shopkeeper with the broken till?

Top tip ⭐

Visit a local shop for the children to see the role of the shopkeeper.

✚ Health & Safety

Ensure adult supervision when children are using small objects such as coins.

Travel agent

What you need:

- Travel agent's role play area made from small gazebo covered in paper and decorated
- Areas to represent a Passport Office and Bureau de Change
- A teddy bear

Role play items such as:

- Travel brochures
- Globe
- Maps
- Telephone
- Suitcases
- Tickets
- Calendars
- Camera
- Computer
- Dressing-up costumes for travel agents, tourists
- Clipboards and writing materials

Non-fiction/fiction books such as:

- *Princess Poppy: The Holiday* by Janey Louise Jones
- *The Funny Fingers are Going on Holiday* by Nikalas Catlow

Taking it forward

To extend their play, suggest some problem-solving scenarios to the children such as the customer has received a letter to say the hotel they booked has closed; the Bureau de Change has no foreign currency left; there is a mistake on a customer's train ticket.

What's in it for the children?

The travel agents role play area develops the children's everyday language relating to money and numbers.

Questions you could ask

- Can we find a different hotel to replace the one that has closed?
- How can we get more foreign currency?
- What should we do about the train ticket that has the wrong time on it?

What to do:

1. Present the children with a suitcase and a teddy called Trevor. Tell the children he is planning to travel around the world. Trevor can 'return' after a few days from his holidays and talk to the children about where he has been and what he has seen. Inform the children that they will be in charge of booking new holidays for Trevor. Using the new role play area, model the whole process of booking a holiday for him and advising him on what he might need for the right climate.

2. The children could take on the role of the customer or travel agent. They might discuss different destinations, plan holidays or even pack their suitcases (with the dressing up clothes provided). Include a Bureau de Change as this will help the children to become familiar with foreign currency. This is a fantastic role play area for dealing with numbers. The children could write estimates for the cost of the holiday filling out forms, working out dates, timings and even the weight of the luggage.

Top tips ⭐

Take photos of Trevor at various holiday destinations.

Depending on your location, take the children on a visit to a real travel agents.

➕ Health & Safety

Ensure adult supervision ratios are suitable before organising a trip.

Ice cream shop

What you need:

- Ice cream shop role play area made from play structure covered in paper and painted

Role play items such as:

- Pretend ice creams/empty tubs
- Toy fridge
- Dressing-up costumes for shopkeepers, customers
- Toy till and money
- Telephone
- Price list
- Clipboards and writing materials

Non-fiction/fiction books such as:

- *Ice Cream Work* by Naoshi
- *Ice cream Bear* by Jez Alborough

What to do:

1. Introduce the role play area by delivering a special invitation to visit a 'real' ice cream van, kiosk or shop. Give each children a token to order and pay for their own ice cream. Point out to the children that you can tell ice cream van has arrived by the sound of the chimes.

2. The role play area is ideal for the children to negotiate different roles. They might pretend to be the shopkeeper ordering, creating and then selling the different ice creams. Or they could be the customer and pretend to order a selection of different flavoured ice creams.

Taking it forward

To extend their play suggest some problem-solving scenarios to the children such as the shop freezer has broken and needs fixing before all the ice-creams melt; there is no chocolate ice cream left; the boxes of ice cream cones have been dropped and have smashed.

What's in it for the children?

The ice cream shop role play area develops the children's everyday language relating to money and numbers. They can be encouraged to buy and sell a range of items, add up prices and give the correct change.

Questions you could ask

- Who should we phone about the freezer?
- How do we order more chocolate ice cream?
- What should we do about the smashed ice cream cones?

Top tip ⭐

Make a 'wow' invitation for the children by attaching giant ice creams. Create the cone from paper and fill it with blown up balloons.

 Health & Safety

Ensure children have no allergies before trying the different ice creams.

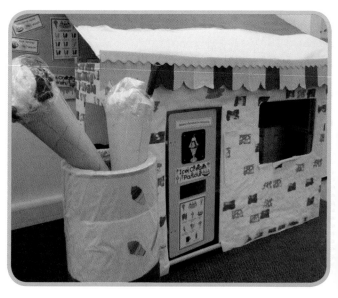

Ice palace

What you need:

- Ice palace role play area made from play tent structure covered in paper and cardboard
- Snowflake sequins

Role play items such as:

- Cups, plates, cutlery
- Menu
- Dressing-up costumes for chef, waiter/waitresses, customers, Jack Frost
- Pretend frozen food
- Order forms
- Toy till and money
- Telephone
- Clipboards and writing materials

Non-fiction/fiction books such as:

- *Here Comes Jack Frost* by Kazuno Kohara
- *The Tale of Jack Frost* by David Melling

What to do:

1. To create excitement around Ice palace café, the children could arrive one morning and investigate a problem. Jack Frost has stolen all the food from the café leaving a note and trails of ice (made out of snowflake sequins). The note explains Jack Frost was hungry and loves frozen food. He heard about their ice palace café and wanted all their food. Let the children decide what action to take next. The children can follow the trail of snowflake sequins to solve the mystery and find Jack with the missing food. They could suggest ways to punish Jack Frost for stealing all the food.

2. The children could take on the role of the waiter, waitress, chef or the customer. They could take orders, write out the bills, cook the food or order and eat the food. As this is the ice palace café the children could order and eat only frozen food such as chicken nuggets, fish fingers, or iced tea.

Taking it forward

To extend their play suggest some problem-solving scenarios to the children such as the customer is angry that their food is cold; the waiter drops the tray of food all over the customer; the chef has run out of chips and customers has ordered them.

What's in it for the children?

The ice palace café role play area will develop the children's everyday language relating to money and numbers. They can be encouraged to buy and sell a range of items, add up prices and give the correct change.

Questions you could ask

- How do you think we can calm the customer down?
- What can you do to help clean up the customer?
- What are we going to say to the customer?

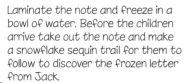

Top tip

Laminate the note and freeze in a bowl of water. Before the children arrive take out the note and make a snowflake sequin trail for them to follow to discover the frozen letter from Jack.

Garage

What you need:

- Car garages made from play structures and decorated.

Role play items such as:

- Tools and toolbox
- Toy petrol pump
- Wheeled toys
- **Ramp** (made from large wooden blocks)
- Cloths
- Polish
- Plastic oil cans
- Paint brushes
- Car manuals
- Telephone
- Hosepipe
- Computer
- Toy till and money
- Bucket and sponge
- Dressing-up costumes for mechanics, customers, a receptionist
- Clipboards and writing materials

Non-fiction/fiction books such as:

- *Cool Cars* by Tony Mitton
- *The Life of a Car* by Susan Steggall

What's in it for the children?

The children will develop their communication and language skills by suggesting ways to solve problems, initiating ideas and then responding to what others are saying. They will also develop their physical skills by using the tools and equipment effectively.

Questions you could ask

- Why is the car making that strange sound? How can we stop it?
- What can we do to help the driver with a flat tyre?
- How can we fix the exhaust?

Health & Safety

Ensure adult supervision if children are exploring real tools and materials.

What to do:

1. Your 'wow' factor scenario: when the children go outside they discover one of their toy cars is unsafe. There is a large screw on the floor. It has a message from the caretaker saying that she is too busy to find out where the screw has come from and fix the car but has heard they have their own garage and was wondering if the children would they like to use her tools to try fixing it?

2. The children using this area will take on the role of a car mechanic. They could fix different vehicles. They will need to work together to solve problems. The area could also include a telephone where the receptionist is in charge of taking calls, making bookings and organising quotes.

Taking it forward

To extend their play suggest some problem-solving scenarios to the children such as the car is making a strange noise; a car has a flat tyre and needs towing to the garage; we don't have to correct spanner that we can use to fix the exhaust.

Top tip ⭐

Watch video clips on how to fix car parts.

Visit a real garage or invite a car mechanic in to talk to the children

Army

What you need:

- Army role play areas made from a play tent structure covered in an army-patterned tablecloth and pop up play tent
- A teddy bear

Role play items such as:

- Backpacks
- First aid kits
- Toy soldiers
- Binoculars
- Compasses
- Mobile phones
- Gas masks
- Dressing-up costumes for doctors, nurses, soldiers
- Clipboards and writing materials

Non-fiction/fiction books such as:

- *Hero Dad* by Melinda Hardin
- *H is for Honor* by Devin Scillian

What's in it for the children?

The children will acquire new vocabulary associated with the army and war. They will develop their communication and language skills by initiating ideas and responding to others ideas.

Questions you could ask

- How can we help the soldiers find their way?
- How can the soldier signal for more help?
- How can we help the soldier who is hurt?
- Who can help fix the tank?
- What should we do next?

Top tip

Make costumes to support a planned army day. The practitioners and children could march around the setting pretending to be soldiers.

What to do:

1. The children receive a message. There is a visitor outside waiting for them. A teddy called Clever Connor, a Corporal who works in the army has camped outside overnight waiting for their help. Connor has a note with him. It says, 'Please can you help me I am the squad leader. I have lost all my team members.' With the support of the practitioner the children can decide how to help Clever Connor.

2. The children could pretend to be the soldiers involved in a war. The children could decide on who is fighting and why. They might plan secret escapes or hide outs to look for the enemy or driving the tank to safety. Throughout the children's play a soldier might end up hurt. The doctors and nurses would take on the role to care for the wounded soldier.

Taking it forward

To extend their play suggest some problem-solving scenarios to the children such as the soldiers are lost; the soldiers have found the enemy but need more help; the tank has broken down.

Hospital

What you need:

- Hospital role play area made from wooden play structure and decorated

Role play items such as:

- Dressing-up costumes for doctors, nurses and patients
- Rubber gloves
- Bandages, plasters, cotton wool
- Medicine bottles, spoons
- Toy/plastic syringes
- Stethoscopes
- Thermometers
- X-ray pictures
- Weighing scales and height charts
- Telephone
- Prescriptions
- Appointment book
- Clipboards and writing material

Non-fiction/fiction books such as:

- *I Don't Want to go to Hospital (Little Princess)* by Tony Ross
- *Hospital (First Time)* by Jess Stockham

What to do:

1. Introduce the role play area of the hospital by telling the children a made up story about a member of staff. Tell the children that they have hurt themselves whilst trying to put the children's work up on a display. They fell off the ladder and have injured their ankle. Explain to the children that they have lost their memory and don't know what to do. Can the children help? Let the children to suggest ideas for how they can help using the equipment and resources in the role-play hospital.

2. The children could take on various roles within the hospital such as pretending to be the doctor, nurse or patient. They might help the patient by checking their blood pressure, heartbeat or pulse. Measuring the patient's weight, height and check their temperature. They will need to record the patient's observations, take x-rays, book appointments, diagnose symptoms and write reports.

Top tip ⭐

Arrange for a nurse or doctor to visit the children and talk about their role.

Use a walking stick as a prop to make the injury more realistic.

50 fantastic ideas for creative role play

Taking it forward

To extend their play suggest some problem-solving scenarios to the children such as they need to write out the patient's prescription but there are no forms; a patient has a high temperature; a patient's leg is x-rayed and found to be broken.

What's in it for the children?

The children will develop their communication and language skills by suggesting ways to solve problems, initiating ideas and then responding to what others are saying. The children will also be able to use their knowledge based on first aid experiences.

Questions you could ask

- How can you write the prescription?
- What do you need to do if the patient has a high temperature?
- How can we make the patient's leg better?

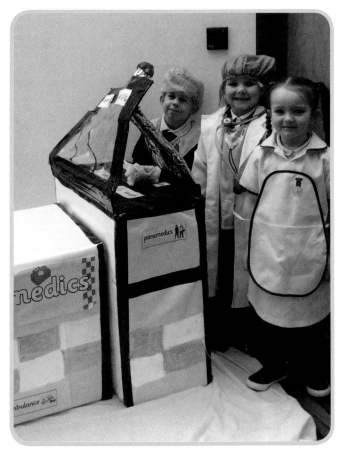

Pirates

What you need:

- Pirate role play area made from small gazebo covered in pirate themed tablecloth.
- Pirate ship made from large sheet cardboard.

Role play items such as:

- Treasure chest filled with toy treasure (plastic jewellery, fake coins etc.)
- Soft toy parrots
- Treasure maps
- Spades
- Compasses
- Telescopes
- Message bottles
- Dressing-up costumes for pirates, sailors, mermaids
- Clipboards and writing materials

Non-fiction/fiction books such as:

- *Ten Little Pirates* by Mike Brownlow
- *Pirate Post* by Ladybird

What to do:

1. To start the topic of pirates show the children a bottle you found on the beach with a message inside from someone asking for help. The message is from a pirate who is lost on an island far away. He needs the children to help rescue him. They need to send him a map of how to get home and send it back to him in a bottle.

2. The children can enjoy taking on the role of pirates, stealing a ship and then making it strong to hold heavy cannons. The children could then sail the ship to find hidden treasure. Provide a treasure map to help the children search for it. Set up various tasks such as steering the ship away from the lighthouse during a storm, capturing prisoners or firing the cannons at the enemy. Don't forget to introduce pirate sayings such as 'Ahoy there me hearties!', 'All hands on deck' and 'Batten down the hatches'.

Taking it forward

To extend their play suggest some problem-solving scenarios to the children such as is there somewhere safe for a 'lookout' on the boat; there is danger on the way; the captain has gone missing and there is no one to take charge; the boat has a leak.

What's in it for the children?

The children will acquire new vocabulary associated with the pirates and ships. They will develop their communication and language skills by initiating ideas and responding to others ideas.

Questions you could ask

- How can you make a safe lookout?
- What can you do without the Captain?
- How can you stop the boat from leaking?

Top tip

Organise a pirate day where the children come dressed as pirates. Follow a treasure hunt, have a pirate picnic and play pirate party games such as 'walk the plank' and 'pin the patch on the pirate'.

Superheroes

What you need:

- Superhero role play area made from a small gazebo covered in superhero tablecloth.
- Superhero parasol covered in paper and decorated with superhero pictures.
- Soft paper to use as 'rope'

Role play items such as:

- Capes
- Masks
- Camera
- Toy guns
- Plastic superhero toys
- Clipboards and writing materials

Non-fiction/fiction books such as:

- *Super Stan* by Matt Robertson
- *Super Ben* by Steve Smallman

What to do:

1. Organise a superhero day where the children and staff come dressed as their favourite super heroes. Start the day by letting the children find a member of staff tied up with paper. There is a note attached to them telling the children a villain has done this and they need to solve the mystery. The villain has stolen all their superhero toys and will keep them until the children work out who the villain is by following the clues.

2. Set up a backdrop scene where the children can acquire super powers and fly or a photo booth for the children to explore becoming different superheroes. Let the children's imaginations run wild by setting up an obstacle course. The children could limbo, shoot rockets at targets, climb through tunnels, and even burst through a wall of cardboard boxes.

3. The children could pretend to be superheroes with super powers like flying, super strength, x-ray vision and supersonic speed. Set up various tasks such as finding the villains, solving problems and rescuing people.

Taking it forward

To extend their play suggest some problem-solving scenarios to the children such as: a superhero has lost their super power; someone is in trouble – can a superhero rescue them using their power; there is a fight between two superheroes.

What's in it for the children?

The children will develop their physical abilities by overcoming obstacles and developing their gross motor skills.

Questions you could ask

- How can you help the superhero get back their magical powers?
- Can you stop the superheroes fighting? How?

Top tip ★

Decorate the gazebo or parasol using superhero wrapping paper.

Airport

What you need:

- Aeroplane structure made from cardboard and decorated with paper.
- Areas to represent check in desk, passport control room and waiting area.

Role play items such as:

- Tickets
- Trolley
- Pretend food and drinks
- Blankets and pillows
- Lifejacket
- Suitcases, luggage labels
- Loudspeaker
- Dressing-up costumes for flight attendant, pilot, passengers
- Clipboards and writing materials

Non-fiction/fiction books such as:

- Airplanes! by Jenny Rive
- George Goes on a Plane by Nicola Smee

What to do:

1. Set up a problem-solving scenario: there has been an incident outside the front of the airport. Some suitcases have fallen out of a passing aeroplane and landed on the ground. The suitcases have luggage labels on them, what should we do? The children can decide what needs to happen next. The children may suggest contacting the police or the pilot.

2. The children could take on the role of a pilot, flight attendant or a passenger. As a flight attendant the children can make announcements, weigh the cases or write out the tickets and itineraries. On the aeroplane the flight attendant could write down the seat number and take drink and snack orders. As a customer they could load up a trolley and order drinks and snacks for the flight.

Taking it forward

To extend their play suggest some problem-solving scenarios to the children such as a plane has a fault; a passenger hasn't paid for their ticket; the flight attendant has spilt a drink over a passenger; some luggage has been lost.

What's in it for the children?

The airport is a great role play area for children to develop their language and communication skills. They will interact with other children, initiate ideas and explore making up stories adding narrative into their play.

Questions you could ask

- How can we fix the aeroplane?
- What should we do with the passenger who hasn't got a ticket?
- Can we help clean up the mess?

Top tips ⭐

Show the children video clips of real airports and what it's like to travel on an aeroplane.

If possible, take the children on a trip to an airport.

Bears

What you need:

- A bear's role play area made from small gazebo covered in paper and decorated. This area could have painted tree stumps, pine cones, fake snow and white material inside.

Role play items such as:

- Tablecloth
- Teddy bears
- Plates and cups
- Party hats
- Balloons
- Dressing-up costumes for bears, explorers
- Clipboards and writing materials

Non-fiction/fiction books such as:

- *We're Going on a Bear Hunt* by Michael Rosen
- *Polar Bear, Polar Bear, What Do You Hear?* by Eric Carle

What to do:

1. Create excitement by setting up teddy bear paw prints leading to a giant teddy bear. The bear could be looking sad holding an empty pot of honey; he has eaten his last jar of honey. Invite the children to suggest ideas for what they could do to help the bear. Suggest that teddy bears like picnics and that they could invite him to their picnic. The children could bring their own teddy bears to the picnic too. Help the children to plan and prepare the teddy bears' picnic.

2. The children could pretend to go on an adventure searching for a bear. This could directly link to the book *We're Going on a Bear Hunt* by Michael Rosen. The children could imagine they are going through the grass, woods, mud, snow storms and finally into the cave. The children could also dress up their teddy bears for different weather conditions and go on a parade.

Taking it forward

To extend their play suggest some problem-solving scenarios to the children such as the bear is missing; the bear is unhappy; the bear wants to be our friend.

What's in it for the children?

The children will develop their communication and language skills by suggesting ways to solve problems, initiating ideas and then responding to what others are saying.

Questions you could ask

- How can we find the bear?
- What should we do to make the bear happy?
- What should we do with our new friend the bear?

Top tip ⭐

To introduce the traditional story of Goldilocks and the Three Bears provide props for retelling the story. Next the children can act out the story themselves.

Pizza shop

What you need:

- Pizza role play area made from small gazebo covered in paper and decorated

Role play items such as:

- Takeaway boxes
- Telephone
- Toy till and money
- Dressing-up costumes for chef, waiter/waitress, customers
- Menus
- Pretend food
- Pizza trays
- Pizza cutter
- Oven
- Clipboards and writing materials

Non-fiction/fiction books such as:

- *How to Make a Pizza* by Zoe Clarke
- *Counting On Pizza!* by Mike Gowar

What to do:

1. Set up a problem-solving scenario ready for the children's arrival. The children could be faced with a mess in the pizza shop. Someone has left a note telling the children they have stolen the pizzas and their secret recipe for tomato sauce. Prepare the pizza shop with the till pulled open, boxes, costumes and food all over the floor. The children have to solve the problem and decide what to do next.

2. The children can take on the role of pizza shop chef and prepare and cook the pizza to order. They could take phone calls, pretend to deliver the pizzas or be the customer and make an order.

3. The children could be involved in designing and making their own pizzas.

Top tip ⭐

Use collage materials to make toppings for the pizzas. Make an oven using a cardboard box and foil. Use wooden logs and coloured paper for the fire.

Taking it forward

To extend their play suggest some problem-solving scenarios to the children such as thy have taken down the wrong house number for the pizza delivery; when the pizza is delivered it is the wrong pizza; the moped runs out of petrol when en route to deliver the pizza.

What's in it for the children?

The pizza shop role play area will develop the children's everyday language relating to money and numbers. They will be encouraged to buy and sell a range of pizzas. They will engage in imaginative role play based on their own experiences.

Questions you could ask

■ What might you do if the chef has given you the wrong house number?
■ How can you help the customer get the correct pizza?
■ What could you do to get more petrol for the mo-ped?

Monsters

What you need:

- A monster role play den made from a pop-up tent covered in grey scrunched paper and then painted
- Stencil monster footprints
- Pretend slime

Role play items such as:

- Soft toy monsters
- Monster masks and costumes
- Cages with padlocks and keys
- Magnifying glasses
- Clipboards and writing materials

Non-fiction/fiction books such as:

- *How to Catch a Monster* by Michael Yu
- *The Very Helpful Monsters* by Sally Huss

Questions you could ask

- How can we find the monster?
- How can we find out which monster has eaten the snack?
- Where might the monster be?

Top tip

Create a cage by covering a large cardboard box in tin foil and adding a huge lock and key. Make monster detective hats and provide magnifying glasses for the children to take on the role of detectives.

What to do:

1. Set monster footprints around the setting leading to a large cage. Inside there is a monster! Encourage the children to suggest ideas for what they should do with the monster, what she might eat and where she should live.

2. Provide a den for the children to pretend to be monsters. They could take on the role of a friendly or nasty monster. Over a series of days the monsters in the setting could be involved in making a 'monster mess' or breaking things. The children can then solve the mysteries and decide what to do with each monster. The children will enjoy inventing new monsters with special powers, too.

Taking it forward

To extend their play suggest some problem-solving scenarios to the children such as the monster has escaped from the cage; a monster has eaten all their snacks; the monster has disappeared.

What's in it for the children?

This role play area will stimulate the children's imagination. The children can develop their communication and language skills by suggesting ways to solve problems, initiating ideas and then responding to what others are saying.

Witches

What you need:

- Witches' cave role play area made from play structure covered in paper and decorated.

Role play items such as:

- Cauldron
- A 'mystery magic box' (cardboard box covered in shiny paper)
- Soft and plastic toy animals
- Broomsticks
- Magic spoon
- Dressing-up costumes for witches, wizards, cats
- Clipboards and writing materials

Non-fiction/fiction books such as:

- *The Witches Big Night* by Sally Huss
- *The Witch with an Itch* by Helen Baugh

Taking it forward

To extend their play suggest some problem-solving scenarios to the children such as a witch has lost her broomstick; a witch is poorly and lost her magic powers; there are pages missing from the witches' spell book.

What's in it for the children?

This role play area will stimulate the children's imagination. They will develop their communication and language skills by suggesting ways to solve problems, initiating ideas and responding to what others are saying.

Questions you could ask

- I wonder if the witch's broomstick is near here. What do you think?
- How can we help the witch get back her magical powers?
- What can we do without the pages from the spell book?

What to do:

1. Fill a large, sparkly box containing a cauldron, spoon and a letter from 'Wilmer the Witch' for the children to discover when they arrive in the setting. Read the letter aloud; Wilmer needs the children to cast a magic spell for her! They must fill her cauldron with objects that rhyme, and mix them together with the magic spoon. What do the children think the spell will do?

2. The children could pretend to be a witch, wizard or witch's cat. They could make up spells and add items to their potions. They could record their spells in the spell book. Or the children could simply enjoy pretending to be witches flying on their broomsticks around the outside area.

Top tip ⭐

Create a fire for the cauldron to stand on using logs, fairy lights and coloured paper.

Castles

What you need:

- Castle role play area made from large cardboard sheets and painted
- Runner bean seeds
- Soil
- Seed trays
- Bean plants

Role play items such as:

- Swords
- Hobby horse
- Shields
- Magic wands
- Jewellery
- Dressing-up costumes for fairy tale characters
- Clipboards and writing materials

Non-fiction/fiction books such as:

- *Castles Picture Book* by Abigail Wheatley
- *The Kiss That Missed* by David Melling

What to do:

1. The children receive a special letter from Jack. He tells them that the other day he found some magic beans in the corner of his garden. He has sent them to the children, to plant and see how much they grow. Together with the children plant the beans and watch them grow. You could have some already grown bean plants that the children haven't seen and replace them the next day so they think the beans are magic and growing extra fast!

2. Provide dressing-up costumes such as king, queen, prince, princess, knight, wizard, witch, fairy, elves and dragons. Act out other well known traditional tales that involve a castle. Make up fantasy stories that include good and evil sides such as a knight rescuing a princess (or prince) in distress.

Taking it forward

To extend their play suggest some problem-solving scenarios to the children such as all the queens' jewellery has gone missing; a wicked witch has put a spell on the princess; a dragon is in trouble it is trapped and needs your help.

What's in it for the children?

The children will develop their communication and language skills by suggesting ways to solve problems, initiating ideas and responding to what others are saying.

Questions you could ask

- How can we help the queen find her stolen jewellery?
- I wonder how we can reverse the spell from the witch?
- How can we help rescue the dragon?

Top tip

Paint the beans with brightly coloured paint and add glitter so the children think they are magic.

✚ Health & Safety

Ensure adult supervision when children are using small objects such as beans.

Celebration shop

What you need:

- Celebration role play area made from a decorated canopy
- A helium balloon

Role play items such as:

- Gift bags
- Wrapped presents
- Party hats and decorations
- Price tags
- Toy till and money
- Telephone
- Dressing-up costumes for shopkeepers, customers
- Clipboards and writing materials

Non-fiction/fiction books such as:

- *The Birthday Party* by Helen Oxenbury
- *My Birthday Party* by Barrie Wade

Questions you could ask

- How can you help the customer find the correct size bag?
- What do we need to do to get more party hats?
- What should we do about the gift bags?

Health & Safety

Ensure adult supervision when children are using small objects such as coins.

What to do:

1. Open the shop with a special event such as the children planning a real birthday party for someone in their class. The children could receive a special invitation tied to a helium balloon. The invitation could be from the party princess who has heard about their fantastic celebration shop and wants them to plan a special party for themselves and invite her. With support the children could plan and organise a party.

2. Invite the children to become the shopkeeper where they can serve the customers. They could also take on the role of the customer and request different items.

Taking it forward

To extend their play suggest some problem-solving scenarios to the children such as the customer has a gift of a certain size that requires a gift bag; the shop has sold the last party hat; the gift bags are faulty.

What's in it for the children?

- The celebration shop role play area will develop the children's everyday language relating to money and numbers. The children will need to ask for the different prices, sizes and weights of different items.

Top tip ⭐

Provide wrapped presents and gift bags of different sizes and weight for the children to explore.

Wild West

What you need:

- Wild West role play area made from small gazebo covered in paper and decorated with giant feathers.
- Role play canoe made from cardboard and then painted.

Role play items such as:

- Hobbyhorse
- Wanted posters
- Straw bales
- Horse shoes
- Fishing rods and toy fish
- Sieves
- Gold
- Sand
- Tin cans
- Rope for lassos
- Dressing-up costumes for Native Americans, cowboys/cowgirls, the sheriff
- Clipboards and writing materials

Non-fiction/fiction books such as:

- *Cowboy!* by Meg Clibbon
- *Cowboys* by Lucille Recht Penner

What to do:

1. Prepare the children to go wild about the Wild West! They need to take part in a series of activities to become the Chief Cowboy of Kentucky. They could take part in various challenges such as: apple bobbing, finding the lost gold mine, panning for gold, lassoing a pony or a tin can.

2. The children could take on the role of a cowboy/girl. They could look after the cattle on the ranch or they could use fishing roads and nets to catch fish for tea. The children could create a campfire to cook the fish.

3. Support the children in making a jail using a large box with brick prints over it and bars for the window. Decorate the setting with 'wanted' posters. Organise an area where the children can explore panning for gold. They could scoop sand up to find pennies or gold.

Top tip

Create a 'wanted' photo booth for the children to experience becoming different Wild West cowboy characters using nicknames such as Snake-eyes, Saddlesore, King Rooster or Six Gun Dizzy.

✚ Health & Safety

Ensure children wash their hands after touching sand.

Taking it forward

To extend their play suggest some problem-solving scenarios to the children such as there is threat of a wolf killing the cattle; the Cowboy King Rooster has escaped from the jail; there is a hole in the bag of gold and some is missing.

What's in it for the children?

The children will develop their communication and language skills by suggesting ways to solve problems, initiating ideas and then responding to what others are saying.

Questions you could ask

- What can we do to save the cattle from the wolf?
- How can we find the Cowboy King Rooster?
- Where do you think the gold is?

Police

What you need:

- Police station structure made from a garden archway covered in paper and decorated
- A jail made from a large cardboard sheet and painted

Role play items such as:

- Handcuffs
- Telephone
- Walkie-talkie
- Fingerprint making kit
- Wanted posters
- Report book
- Prison keys
- Dressing-up costumes for police officers, criminals
- Clipboards and writing materials

Non-fiction/fiction books such as:

- *Police Officer* by Amanda Askew
- *A Day at the Police Station* by Richard Scarry

What to do:

1. The children come into the setting and the phone rings: it's a police officer informing that they have just caught a criminal and they are on their way to put them into the cell. But oh no! The prison cell keys have gone missing! Let the children decide what to do next.

2. Use the outdoor area to allow the children more space to capture the criminals. Set up scenarios such an emergency call; a criminal has just been caught and they need back up. They could make up their own clues and endings.

Taking it forward

To extend their play suggest some problem-solving scenarios to the children such as the teacher's car has been stolen; the window has been smashed; there has been a car crash and there's lots of traffic.

What's in it for the children?

The children will develop their communication and language skills by suggesting ways to solve problems, initiating ideas and then responding to what others are saying.

Questions you could ask

- How can we find the person who stole the car?
- Are there any clues as to who smashed the window?
- How can we stop the traffic?

Top tip ★

To introduce the new role play area try to visit a real police station or have a visitor from the police force. They could even use the vehicles!

Fire station

What you need:

- Fire engine made from play structure frame and covered in paper and decorated

Role play items such as:

- Fire extinguishers
- Firefighter costumes
- Walkie-talkies
- Megaphone
- Hose
- Fire blankets
- Ladder
- Buckets
- Hose
- Clipboards and writing materials

Non-fiction/fiction books such as:

- *Emergency! (Awesome Engines)* by Margaret Mayo

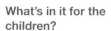

What's in it for the children?

The children will develop their communication and language skills by suggesting ways to solve problems, initiating ideas and responding to what others are saying.

Questions you could ask

- What are you going to do to fix the fire engine?
- How can we drive the fire engine?
- How can we get more water for the fire engine?

Top tip ⭐

Record fire engine and telephone ringing noises onto sound buttons so the children can use them as and when they need to in their play.

What to do:

1. To introduce the new role play area try to visit a real fire station or see a fire engine. Enquire whether you can borrow a real firefighter's uniform for the children to investigate.

2. Make the area fun by having races between the children to see who can get ready as a firefighter first. Hide the different parts of the uniform around the setting, the quickest firefighter could become the crew or station manager. Create flames made of red, yellow and orange paper stuck to a cardboard townscape then surprise the children by setting off a small fire alarm. The children can take on the roles of the firefighters and pretend to put out the fire.

3. Set up scenarios such as the phone could ring in the fire station area with an emergency call; a cat is stuck in a tree – can they rescue it? Find a large cardboard box and use paint to turn it into a fire engine for the children to drive.

Taking it forward

To extend their play suggest some problem-solving scenarios to the children such as a fire engine has broken down; the firefighter who drives the fire engine is ill; the fire engine is out of water.

Post Office

What you need:

- Post office role play area created from a large cardboard sheet that's been decorated

Role play items such as:

- Post bags and parcel sacks
- Safe
- Toy till and money
- Telephone
- Weighing scales
- Brown wrapping paper
- Parcels and envelopes
- Post box
- Dressing-up costumes for post workers, customers
- Clipboards and writing materials

Non-fiction/fiction books such as:

- *Will Goes to the Post Office* by Olof and Lena Landstrom
- *Out and About at the Post Office* by Becky Shipe

Taking it forward

To extend their play suggest some problem-solving scenarios to the children such as the weighing scales are faulty; the post office has run out of envelopes; a mysterious parcel has arrived at the post office without a name and address.

What's in it for the children?

The children will develop their communication and language skills by suggesting ways to solve problems, initiating ideas and then responding to what others are saying. The children will also be able to use their knowledge based on first hand experiences.

Questions you could ask

- What should we do to fix the weighing scales?
- How can we order more envelopes?
- What should we do about the mysterious parcel?

What to do:

1. Introduce the area of the post office by presenting a problem-solving scenario to the children. Set up the role play area with plastic money all over the floor and an open safe. Inform the children that the post office has been burgled and they have arrived just in time. The burglar was in such a rush he dropped the money all over the floor. The children can decide what to do next to catch the burglar and work out if all the money is still safe.

2. The children could take on the role of the customer or post office worker. The customers could bring parcels and letters to post. They could write addresses, fill out forms and handle money. The post office worker would need to weigh parcels, answer the telephone and sort letters.

Top tip ⭐

Create a safe out of a cardboard box and cover it with foil. Scatter plastic money in the safe and all over the floor.

Construction site

What you need:

- Construction role play area made from small gazebo covered in paper and decorated

Role play items such as:

- Wooden blocks
- Pretend tools
- Cones
- Builder costumes
- Pipes and tubes
- Building plans
- Clipboards and writing materials

Non-fiction/fiction books such as:

- *Goodnight, Goodnight, Construction Site* by Sherri Duskey Rinker
- *Let's Explore the Construction Site* by Baby Professor

What to do:

1. In preparation, explain to the children a new construction area will be created that night as a builder needs help to putting some fencing up. The next morning, explain to the children that they cannot use the area yet because the builder has been very untidy and he has left all his tools around the setting. Show the children a list of the missing tools are: they will be eager to help and search for them. For added interest and excitement, play suitable 'building' music whilst the children hunt for the tools.

2. The children using this area will take on the role of construction workers. They could build different structures, buildings, roads, houses, castles, palaces or dens. To build these structures they will need to work together to join different materials, construct roofs and walls. The area could also include a telephone where the site manager is in charge of designing new building projects and giving quotes to new customers.

Taking it forward

To extend their play suggest some problem-solving scenarios to the children such as a letter from the Queen ordering the children to build a new palace; overnight the wind had blown down a house; the school needs an extension as more children need a place.

What's in it for the children?

The children will develop their communication and language skills by suggesting ways to solve problems, initiating ideas and then responding to what others are saying. They will also develop their physical skills by using the tools and equipment effectively.

Questions you could ask

- How do we build a palace?
- Can we fix the house that has blown down?
- What materials do they need to extend the school?

Top tip

Provide exciting stimuli by adding real household objects such as light switches, wires, pipes, door locks and wood to extend the children's creative thinking.

➕ Health & Safety

Ensure adult supervision if children are exploring real tools and materials.

What you need:

- Healthy eating café made from a play tent structure covered in paper and cardboard

Role play items such as:

- Cutlery, plates, cups
- Picnic hamper/basket
- Dressing-up costumes for chef, waiter/waitress, customers
- Menu
- Toy till and money
- Play food (including plastic fruit and veg)
- Order forms
- Menus
- Telephone
- Clipboards and writing materials

Non-fiction/fiction books such as:

- *Healthy Eating* by Deborah Chancellor
- *Yummy Stories: Fruits, Vegetables and Healthy Eating Habits* by Lil Alexander

What to do:

1. Set up a problem for the new healthy eating café. Tell the children when you were setting up the area you discovered all the play food has gone missing. The café can't open without food. Invite the children to put forward suggestions for what to do. An idea would be to inform the headteacher or manager of the setting. The next day the children could receive a present of a large hamper full of food- but something is wrong! In the hamper there is healthy and unhealthy food. The headteacher/manager thought it was just a café and didn't realise we only need healthy food. Support the children to sort the food ready to open the café. They could also write a letter to the headteacher/manager to thank them for the hamper.

2. Initially children will need to discuss what role they will to take on while using the café. They might choose to be the chef, waiter, waitress or a customer. They could take orders, prepare the food and then serve it to the customer. This area will provide opportunities for the children to serve healthy and unhealthy food and encourage discussion into what is a healthy choice. Support the children to create their own menu for their café.

Top tip ⭐

Use this area not only to serve play food but real healthy snacks too.

Taking it forward

To extend their play suggest some problem-solving scenarios to the children such as the fridge is over full and another delivery has just arrived; a customer has ordered a banana and they have sold out; a customer has forgotten their purse.

What's in it for the children?

The children will be introduced to healthy eating and learn what makes a healthy diet. They will learn new key vocabulary to support their play in this area.

Questions you could ask

- What should we do with all the extra food?
- What should we say to the customer?
- How can the customer pay?

Film studio

What you need:

- Film studio back drop made from large cardboard sheets and decorated

Role play items such as:

- Director's chair
- Clapperboard
- Film reel
- Video camera
- Microphone
- Scripts
- Awards
- Red carpet
- Loudspeaker
- Dressing-up costumes for directors, sound technicians, film stars and characters
- Clipboards and writing materials

What to do:

1. To celebrate the achievements of the children, use this area to organise an award ceremony. Surprise the children on arrival to the setting with a red carpet entrance and play 'award night' music. Present the children with a list of nominees for each category such as best director, actor, actress, producer, cameraman and scriptwriter.

2. Set up a stage area and director's chair where the children can take on the role of the director using the clapperboard and loudspeaker. The children could write the film script, plan and then carry out the recording of a movie scene. All the cast, crew, cameraman and soundman will all need direction and have different roles to play.

Taking it forward

To extend their play suggest some problem-solving scenarios to the children such as the script has gone missing; the lead actress lost her voice; a stunt man is seriously hurt.

What's in it for the children?

The film studio role play area will introduce storyline and narrative into their play. The children will learn new vocabulary to support their play in this area. They will develop their communication and language skills by initiating their own and responding to others' ideas.

Questions you could ask

- How can we find the script?
- What should we do? Who can replace the lead actress?
- How can we help the stunt man?

Top tip

Decorate the area with black material and golden stars to create instant showtime impact.

Boats

What you need:

- Boat role play area made from play tent structure covered in cardboard and painted

Role play items such as:

- Wooden blocks
- Plastic sea creatures
- Seashells and pebbles
- Rubber rings
- Fishing nets
- Suitcases
- Telescope
- Compass
- Dressing-up costumes for the captain, sailors, tourists
- Clipboards and writing materials

Non-fiction/fiction books such as:

- *Busy Boats* by Susan Steggall
- *Who Sank the Boat?* by Pamela Allen

What's in it for the children?

This is a great role play area for children to develop their communication and language. They will interact with other children, initiate ideas and explore making up stories, adding narrative into their play.

Questions you could ask

- How can we fix the leak?
- What can we do to free the anchor?
- How can we keep the boat safe?

Top tips

The type and purpose of boat can easily be changed. Try adding props or signs to change it into a fishing boat, lifeboat, ferry, or even a cruise liner – the play opportunities are endless.

Try visiting the seaside or river for the children to experience real boats.

What to do:

1. To start the topic on boats make your chosen boat overnight and then cover it with spare material. Present the children with a special bag containing a gold magic telescope and a photograph of Kamal the Clever Captain. Tell the children the telescope belongs to Kamal and he has given it to them to use and help them find the way to rescue him. Kamal sadly, is stranded on a desert island. After the introduction reveal Kamal's boat to the children and support them to find the way to the island to rescue Kamal. Don't forget to use Kamal's magic telescope.

2. The children can take on the roles of the captain, cabin crew, helmsmen, sailor, pilot or steward. They could initially prepare to go aboard the boat by putting on life jackets and their uniforms and deciding on their roles. The children could explore going on a journey to rescue people, a fishing expedition, hunting for treasure or becoming passengers on a holiday trip around the world.

Taking it forward

To extend their play suggest some problem-solving scenarios to the children such as the boat has a leak; the anchor is caught on something; the storm is bad and the boat is near the rocks.

Bus

What you need:

- Bus role play area made from play tent structure covered in paper and painted

Role play items such as:

- Tickets
- Bags and purses
- Money
- Walkie-talkie
- Maps
- Dressing-up costumes for the bus driver, ticket collector, passengers
- Clipboards and writing materials

Non-fiction/fiction books such as:

- *The Bus is For Us* by Michael Rosen
- *Naughty Bus* by Jan and Jerry Oke

Taking it forward

To extend their play suggest some problem-solving scenarios such as a passenger has got on the wrong bus; a passenger has got on the bus without a ticket; the bus has run out of diesel.

What's in it for the children?

This a great role play area for children to develop their language and communication skills. They will interact with other children, initiate ideas and explore making up stories, adding narrative into their play.

Questions you could ask

- How can we help the passenger find the correct bus?
- What should we do with the passenger who has no ticket?
- How can we get more diesel for the bus?

What to do:

1. Set up a scenario ready for the children for when they come in. Present them with a lost bag that has been left on the bus. Inside is a lady's purse with her address in it and a map. The children have to 'drive' the bus to the lady's house. They will enjoy pretending to follow a map to find her house to return her bag.

2. Encourage them to take on the role of the bus driver or a passenger. The children could line up at the bus stop, steer the bus, press the horn, write and collect the tickets and give change. The children could use a walkie-talkie to communicate with the depot. The children may also want to imagine they are the ticket inspector and check all the passengers' tickets. They could decide where the bus is going and talk about what they pass on the way.

Top tip

Use a CD player in this area for the children to play sound effects of a real bus.
Organise a real trip on a bus so the children can experience what it is really like.

Campsite

What you need:

- Campsite role play area created by using a pop-up tent

Role play items such as:

- Soft toy animals
- Backpacks including torches, maps, compasses
- Sleeping bags
- Picnic rug
- Pretend campfire/ barbeque
- Rubber dinghy fishing boat
- Fishing nets and rods
- First aid kit
- Plastic minibeasts
- Dressing-up costumes for explorers, animals
- Clipboards and writing materials

Non-fiction/fiction books such as:

- *Camping Out* by Heather Amery

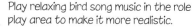

Top tip ⭐

Play relaxing bird song music in the role play area to make it more realistic.

What's in it for the children?

The children will develop their communication and language skills by suggesting ways to solve problems, initiating ideas and then responding to what others are saying. They will also develop their physical skills by using the equipment effectively.

Questions you could ask

- How can we find our way back to the campsite with no map?
- The boat is leaking what can we do?
- Who can help us put out the fire?

➕ Health & Safety

If camping outside ensure children wash their hands after exploring.

What to do:

1. Present the children with a big sack of exciting camping resources and share them. Explain that they are going on a camping expedition and that they need to prepare. Write a list of items needed for a camping adventure and share this with the children, they can check that they have everything. Next write a message on your door to let people know you have all gone camping.

2. The children can take on the role of a camper. They could hike around the setting travelling through challenging landscapes or role-play fishing using the rubber dinghy fishing boat to bring home something for tea. The children will love to imagine having a barbeque for tea, roasting marshmallows over the campfire or even sleeping under the stars. Provide bird and minibeast hunting challenges and record sheets so the children develop can explore outside and to their recording skills.

Taking it forward

To extend their play suggest some problem-solving scenarios to the children such as they get lost going hiking; the boat leaks when they are fishing; the campfire sets the tent on fire.

Seaside

What you need:

- Seaside role play area made from small gazebo covered in paper and decorated. Create the seaside by placing children's picnic chairs and a parasol over yellow material.

Role play items such as:

- Picnic blanket
- Beach balls
- Arm bands, rubber rings
- Life jackets
- Snorkels
- Beach towels
- Fishing rods and nets
- Beach bags
- Bucket and spade
- Shells
- Rubber dingy
- Dressing-up costumes for lifeguards, fishermen, tourists
- Clipboards and writing materials

Non-fiction/fiction books such as:

- *Seaside Poems* by Jill Bennett
- *Theo at the Seaside* by Jaclyn Crupi

Top tips

Use shredded coloured paper as water in the paddling pool. Add natural hessian material for sand.

Depending on your location organise a trip to the seaside.

✚ Health & Safety

Ensure adult supervision ratios are suitable and be aware of the dangers of water with young children.

What to do:

1. To introduce the theme of the seaside surprise the children with a boat full of objects. Explain you visited the seaside at the weekend and bought lots of objects for their new role play area and on the way to school other objects in your car rolled into the boat. The children could look closely at the objects and talk about what they are used for. They could suggest why some of the objects don't belong in the boat.

2. Before using the seaside area the children could prepare to go on holiday or the beach by packing for a holiday. Once 'on holiday' they could build sand castles, have a picnic, take on the role of a lifeguard, pretend to swim in the ocean, surf on the waves or enjoy a beach party.

Taking it forward

To extend their play suggest some problem-solving scenarios to the children such as no lifeguard on the beach and there is a person in trouble in the water; the sand is too hot to walk across and they have lost their shoes; there is a shark in the water!

What's in it for the children?

The children will develop their communication and language skills by suggesting ways to solve problems, initiating ideas and then responding to what others are saying. The children will develop their understanding of the natural world and will develop their ability to talk about the things they learn about the seaside.

Questions you could ask

- How can we find the lifeguard?
- Is there a way we can get back to the hotel without our shoes?
- How can we stay safe when there is a shark in the water?

Under the sea

What you need:

- Gazebo

Role play items such as:

- Parasol and play structure
- Shells
- Plastic fish
- Bucket and spade
- Rubber ring
- Paddling pool
- Snorkel
- Sand
- Fishing nets
- Bubble machine
- Musical instruments
- Under the sea sound effects
- Clipboards and writing materials

Non-fiction/fiction books such as:

- *The Sea* by Marie Aubinais
- *Oceans Tales* by Gail Kisnorbo

Taking it forward

To extend their play suggest some problem-solving scenarios to the children such as a mermaid has a cut on her tail; all the fish are in danger of the sharks; the dolphins are caught in the net.

What's in it for the children?

The children will develop their communication and language skills by suggesting ways to solve problems, initiating ideas and responding to what others are saying. The children will develop their understanding of the natural world and will develop their ability to talk about the creatures that live under the sea.

Questions you could ask

- How can we help the mermaid?
- What should we do about the sharks?
- How can we free the dolphins?

What to do:

1. Excite the children by introducing the under the sea theme by presenting a special friend, Tess the Turtle. She could arrive in special carrier holding an invitation. Explain to the children that she has invited them to her marvellous party and they need to all prepare for the party by finding out as much as they can about living under the sea. The children could research what it's like under the sea. Celebrate the children's learning by rewarding them with a mermaid party.

2. Share the book in 'Reading Under the Reef'. The children can use the role play area to explore books about different sea creatures and what it's like living under the sea. They could spot the different creatures and talk about their different features.

Top tips

For added interest in the area set up a bubble machine.

Depending on your location try taking the children on a trip to a sealife centre.

Submarine

What you need:

- Submarine role play area made from play tent structure covered in paper and cardboard and painted
- A teddy bear

Role play items such as:

- Lifejackets
- Rubber rings
- Seashells
- Fishing nets
- Snorkels
- Suitcases
- Plastic sea creatures
- Dressing-up costumes for the captain, sailing crew
- Clipboards and writing materials

Non-fiction/fiction books such as:

- *Jack's Mega Machines: Supersonic Submarine* by Alison Ritchie
- *Submarine: Picture Book* by Planet Collection

What to do:

1. Show the children photographs of Suki the teddy at the seaside. Explain to the children that you met her at the weekend and she told you she loves sailing her boat on the sea. She is so good she is in charge of sailing a submarine to Somerset on Saturdays and Sundays. But she has a problem and needs your help. The other day she had a visitor, Sadiq the snake and he wanted to go on the submarine too. He brought his suitcase with him but sadly he was not allowed aboard the submarine as some of the items in his suitcase didn't start with 's'. Children love to solve a problem that helps someone so invite them to sort the items and help Sadiq the snake.

2. The children can take on the role of the admiral, captain or lieutenant. They could initially prepare to go on board the submarine, putting on life jackets and their uniforms and deciding on their roles. The children could explore going on a journey to save people and discover hidden treasures under the sea.

Top tips

Laminate pictures of sea creatures for the children to use in the area to encourage new vocabulary and the understanding of alliteration such as seahorse, silver dollar fish, seal, sea dragon, sea lion, salmon and stingray. Or even extend the children's learning of the sound 's' by letting them experience real seaweed, salmon, sprats and sardines.

Taking it forward

To extend their play suggest some problem-solving scenarios to the children such as the submarine has a leak; a giant whale won't move out of the way; the captain is ill.

What's in it for the children?

The children will develop their communication and language skills by suggesting ways to solve problems, initiating ideas and then responding to what others are saying. The children will develop their understanding of the natural world and will develop their ability to talk about the things they have learned about creatures that live under the sea.

Questions you could ask

- How can you stop the leak? What could you do?
- How are you going to move the whale?
- What can we give the captain to make him better?

Traditional stories

What you need:

- The Three Little Pigs role play areas made from decorated pop-up tents, small gazebos and wooden play structures

Role play items such as:

- Masks
- Puppets
- Sticks
- Bricks/wooden blocks
- Cooking pot
- Pretend fire
- Building tools
- Straw
- Dressing-up costume for Three Little Pigs, the Wolf
- Clipboards and writing materials

Non-fiction/fiction books such as:

- *The True Story of The Three Little Pigs* by Jon Scieszka
- *The Three Little Wolves and the Big Bad Pig* by Eugene Trivizas

Taking it forward

To extend their play suggest some problem-solving scenarios to the children such as the pigs have no more cement to build the house out of bricks; the wolf has a sore throat and he can't puff anymore; the fire keeps going out before it can boil the pot of water.

What's in it for the children?

These are great role play areas for children to develop their reading skills and language development. They will share stories and interact with other children retelling and acting out the stories. They will become aware of main characters and the way stories are structured.

Questions you could ask

- How can we get more cement?
- Should we help the wolf get better?
- How can we keep the fire going?

What to do:

1. To introduce the story role play areas of the Three Little Pigs prepare a letter from the Big Bad Wolf. The letter tells the children that he is so sad all alone living in his lair, all he wants to do is make friends with the Three Little Pigs. Allow the children to suggest what they could do to help the pigs and the wolf make friends. The children might like to write a letter to the pigs pretending to be the wolf.

2. Using traditional stories is a fabulous way for the children to develop their confidence in role play. Practitioners need to model and demonstrate acting out the story using props and costumes. The children can then take on the role of the three pigs, the wolf, the three pigs' mother or the man who sells the straw, sticks and bricks. If space allows, it is better to have all three houses to use so the children can move onto the next house before the wolf catches them. Organise straw, sticks and bricks for the children to explore building with different materials.

Top tip ⭐

Encourage the children to build the strongest house out of bricks. Provide a trophy for the children or group of children who can design and make the strongest house.

50 fantastic ideas for creative role play